T0165035

Angelic Visits Today

*A True Novel and Autobiography of a Family
Immigrating From Finland Over A Century Ago*

Helmi Schimke

WESTBOW
P R E S S
A DIVISION OF THOMAS NELSON

ISBN: 978-1-4497-3898-3 (sc)
ISBN: 978-1-4497-3897-6 (e)

Library of Congress Control Number: 2012901731

WestBow Press books may be ordered through booksellers or by contacting:

WestBow Press
A Division of Thomas Nelson
1663 Liberty Drive
Bloomington, IN 47403
www.westbowpress.com
1-(866) 928-1240

Author   Helmi L. Schimke
Daughter   Colleen Y. Wildie
Son   Bruce A. Schimke

Printed in the United States of America
WestBow Press rev. date: 2/27/2012

Author Helmi Schimke with
Husband Harvey

CONTENTS

PREFACE - ONE

This true novel begins during the late 1800's and early 1900's, a century ago, when people were immigrating to the new "land of their dreams," the America's, The United States of America!

My Grandparents were no exception, they wanted their new "Dream" too.

It also encompasses my parents lives and their life's circumstances. Portrays both hardships and enjoyments, accomplishments in many ways, and raising a family of four children through the years of "The Great Depression."

I am one of those four children, and am now 87 years old. My parents, of course, have passed away. But, so has my brother and both of my sisters. I am the only one of the family still living.

It has been by a very strong "revelation" from God that I am writing this true novel. His plans are unknown to us, but there has to be a reason, a purpose, so when we feel compelled to do something that we feel is God-led, all we can do is believe and exercise the knowledge and wisdom that God has given us, and be as obedient as possible.

Angels are a major part of this novel! That is also my reason for writing it, and being obedient to God.

This novel is a true family autobiography of real happenings during my lifetime, and of my parents and grandparents lives. Some awesome angelic encounters and visions, some electrifying, courageous experiences, some frightening and enlightening and much more.

PREFACE - TWO

After you have read this book, I hope that it has helped you in your Christian life as much as these events and experiences have helped me in my Christian walk with God; and, even more, in portraying the reality of God and his angels, and their emphasis and commission in our lives.

There are many, many instances of angelic visits and commissions in both the Old Testament and the New Testament. Psalm 91 tells us that God "Charges" his angels to guard us. Since I was a small child, I've heard that we all have a personal guardian angel. That is also what my parents taught me. I do believe that's true. I also believe that they are commissioned by God to do what he desires, visible or invisible, as the situation dictates.

How many times, if you think about situations and instances in your life, you may have just missed an appointment or something similar, because for some reason you were delayed for a few minutes. I do believe that if we really knew how many times those unseen angels have helped us, we would be astonished! Everyone of us has or has had angels working consistently in our lives, helping us, guiding us and our children, without us ever knowing or being aware that they are all around us.

Maybe someday, when we are in our "heavenly journey," we may be used by God in this same way or manner. I really never entertained that thought very much at all until I started to write this book.

The bible tells us that God created the heavens and the earth, and because of his great love, he created mankind, his children. Everyone of us is his child, and we are here for a reason. As a Christian, with faith and love in Him, He will guide us and bless us throughout our lives.

With the "free will" that he has given us, we can accept his way or go our way. But, he still loves us and helps us when we are receptive and call on him in prayer.

He gives us wisdom, guides us, heals us, even to the point of sending his angels (his helpers, his messengers) when he feels it's necessary, which has been the case in this true life's autobiography/novel.

Chapter 1

Immigration from Finland to America

In 1904 my mother and father immigrated to the United States with their parents. Mother was only 4 years old and my father was born on the ship coming over so he became a citizen as his birth place was New York City. They came over from Finland along with many other Finnish people and they all settled in Michigan in a small settlement which was called Kaleva. That was a century ago and Kaleva now has just about every nationality living there. Time certainly changes things.

My mother and father evidently met in this town and were married. My dad's name was Edward and mom's name was Elizabeth. There were four of us children,

John being the oldest, then me, Helmi, and June and Mae being quite a bit younger.

This true novel portrays events that transpired during their lifetime, while building their new home, gathering farm equipment, animals, etc., and doing all the things necessary to start farming.

My Grandparents bought 120 acres of barren property to begin their future in Michigan. They colonized in a beautiful natural wooded setting.

Everyone at that time had to be a farmer, land had to be cleared, creeks had to be dug to drain the wet land, which was a horrendous undertaking to say the least, so that they could begin to plant crops, do their farming, and make a living. It's hard to imagine how they existed under those circumstances. They were a determined people and wanted to be in the new country, which I'm sure they had heard many good things about, or they would not have ventured into such a challenge.

I remember mom telling me that after I had gone to school for three months as a kindergartner, I came home and told her that she didn't have to speak to me in Finnish anymore because I only knew one word in Finnish now and that was Vasara, which is hammer in English. Of course, that wasn't true as I can still speak Finnish today, some eighty years later. Sometimes it's funny the things a person remembers from their childhood. We had about a mile to walk to get to the little country school that also had to be built during those early settlement years.

I also remember another incident that mom told me about when I was about five or six. It was during the cold Michigan winter months. Some years we really had some cold weather and lots of blowing snowstorms. She said that one of the neighbors had brought me home from school inside of his overcoat because it was blowing and snowing so hard that I couldn't walk or find my way home. It wasn't like today with buses to take you to school and bring you home even though you're very young. There are a lot of things that I remember from those early school years, how we played baseball, and what they called Prisoner's Base, which I remember being a lot of fun. I haven't heard it even mentioned since then.

Mother had one sister and one brother. Her sister died when she was twenty-one from pneumonia. Her brother moved to Atlantic City, New Jersey, when he was about that same age. After mother's parents passed away, she purchased the farm from her brother and that is where the four of us children grew up. It was a real life growing experience for all us, basically starting from "scratch" in a new and strange country.

John Edward "Ed" Troppi
Father of Author Helmi (Troppi) Schimke

Chapter 2

Adjusting to A New Lifestyle in America

I'm writing this true novel of my experiences of being brought up in a Christian home on a family farm during the early 1920's and 30's. This was during the years of the "Great Depression." Everyone looked for any means to grow more food for their families and to feed the animals.

My early memories include a time when my father was badly injured dynamiting a new creek to make the land more productive. The back 40 acres were too wet to cultivate and farm. Therefore, it had to be drained in some manner, and the best way to eliminate the wet land was to make a drain, and the only way it could be done was to dynamite a creek for drainage.

Disaster hit when dad was laying the last of 100 sticks of dynamite and someone accidently hit the switch. The explosion blew him into the air and he landed on a stump. Even though I was only seven, I remember him laying in the back bedroom of our farm house and being unconscious for a long time.

My mother called the doctor to come and help him, but the first doctor that came to see him left without treating him, feeling that there was no hope and he wouldn't survive. My mother got a second doctor to come and he did treat him, setting his broken bones. One of his lungs was crushed and never did return to normal. My mom told me that dad did not move at all for two weeks, and then one day mom said she saw him move his eyelids and she then felt that he would live. During those years the doctors came to the homes when it was necessary. As you can tell, this was a very difficult time for our family health-wise and economically.

It took dad about a year before he was able to get around again. He improved but, of course, he was never the same! However, he was very determined and built high exercise bars and forced himself to exercise even with his broken body and pain. After about another year of regular exercise, he was doing pretty well. I can still see those high bars and how he tried to pull himself higher and higher building muscle so that he could do things again. He did live to be 63 years old.

He did have a very faithful and courageous friend, about his age, that helped him a lot. The two of them would study the Bible until early morning hours. I can still see their gestures and hot discussions of the end times and how the Bible prophesies were being fulfilled prior to Jesus coming. It was very interesting to me even though I was so young at the time.

Around the same time in our families life, mom had very serious asthma and was not able to do much, especially with any farm work because of allergies to grain, weeds, etc.

The burdens of the farm work fell mostly on my brother and me. He was about one and a half years older. We milked the cows and pumped the water for the animals. There was no running water then. It all had to be pumped by hand. Believe me, that was a lot of pumping with so many cows and horses to haul water to. I remember how difficult it was to lift the huge one-half bushel size buckets of water up to the horses, as their bin was at least chest high. And then they would hurry to get the water and push down on the bucket which made it even harder.

That was only part of the work-load that had to be done every day and through the rest of the year. A lot

Why would the switch go off when dad was laying the last of 100 sticks of dynamite, why just then? We didn't know much about switches, especially at that time, which was in the 1920's or 1930's. The only one I know of even now is the plunger type which takes quite a bit of fortitude and strength to engage the mechanism to get it started. Anyway, we will never know, but it still seems so unrealistic for such a dangerous situation to take place, and seemingly go off by itself, and at such a time before it was completely set up and ready to engage.

I was around seven years old at the time of the accident and my brother was around nine.

Mom and dad had bought the farm from her brother as it was inherited from mother's parents. Her parents had been farming the 80 acres where the buildings had been built, but the back 40 acres was too wet to be able to cultivate and farm. That was the reason for excavating and digging the creek, so that it could then drain into the larger river that was nearby, so that it would become productive ground. After they were able to cultivate, plant, and harvest from this new land, it was a real blessing as the ground was so fertile. I can still remember how tall the grain was because we used to play hide-and-seek and had such a hard time finding the other person. It was fun, but for dad what a price to pay!

Chapter 3

Finnish Sauna

They have what they call a "Sauna" today, but it is not anything like the original "Finnish Sauna," which, of course, the Finnish people invented. It was a mainstay, a necessity, in the Finnish culture. The Finnish people that immigrated to America brought this heritage with them, and it became a necessity in America as well.

On the farm we had a separate building for our Sauna. It had two separate rooms. One for the bathing part and another room for cooling off and a dressing area. It was probably about 50 feet in back of the house.

The original Sauna stove heating area was built with a barrel type stove with an open area on the top that was then filled with about 3-4" size stones. When the stove was fired up, which was filled with small wood pieces, it became very hot and heated the stones. The stones had to be very hot before the Sauna could be used. Then when bathing began, water was thrown on the stones which created steam and humidity in the room. The room then became very warm or hot and you began to sweat profusely. This, of course, was the whole purpose so a person would be clean on the inside as well as on the outside, by sweating out the toxins that accumulate in the body. The skin is the second largest elimination organ of the body. People that have not experienced this wonderful way of life have no idea how clean you feel afterwards.

Part of the bathing process included cedar branch stimulation. Small cedar branches were tied together resembling a small fan. Then they would use this fan to softly hit the body. This process would invigorate, stimulate, and enhance circulation. It could also benefit a person's health in many other ways. What a great idea that was, free, and so natural. I know it's hard to imagine how it feels when you haven't experienced it. My children too have missed out on some of the pleasures of their heritage. I hope some day they will be able to experience the real pleasures of the original Finnish sauna.

I'm in my late 80's now but remember the Sauna's so well and miss them.

My German husband couldn't take the "heat" so we never had one. I can understand that too because my brother apprised him of his first Sauna. You know brothers, they have to show off, so he probably made it twice as hot as it had to be. My husband thought he was being tortured and never wanted one again. That took care of his Sauna experience, but don't let that discourage you, as they really are a terrific experience and so good for you.

I remember how good, clean and stimulated I felt afterwards. When we were still quite young and when we were all through with the Sauna and dressed, we would run back to the house barefooted in the snow. We thought it was a lot of fun and didn't even feel the cold. Now it makes me shiver when I think about it. Probably because at my age, I can't even keep my feet warm. Well, things do change!

Evidently Saunas were good for us, as my mother's brother lived to be almost 100, living to be 99 years and 6 months old.

He lived in New Jersey most of his life, and worked as a carpenter, siding being his specialty. The outdoors, the exercise, and the good seafood could have contributed to his long life!

A seafood restaurant that he and his family frequented told him that if he made it to 100 years of age, they

the dream it seemed like it took him forever to get to our house. In those days, they used lanterns instead of flashlights like we do today. In the dream the night was so very dark and it seemed as if I was walking with him, although I wasn't. I was just watching him take every step with his lit lantern swinging back and forth with each step.

In the visionary dream, when he finally got to our driveway, he walked in about 20 feet and he just disappeared, just vanished. I could not imagine what happened or where he went. He just wasn't there anymore. It reminded me of lightening – it strikes and then it's gone. I was just dumb-founded and I just sat on the ground. I don't know for how long. People just don't disappear in front of your eyes like that.

I woke up early the next morning, as on the farm there was always so much to do. With mother and father being so incapacitated, all the chores, watering, feeding, and milking the cows, taking care of the horses and the rest of the animals was all up to my brother and me. He was just a year and a half older than I was so he was about 11 or 12 at that time. That was a big load for two kids, but you do what you have to do. We, of course, did not realize at that age that things should even be any different and were glad to do it as we felt so sorry for mom and dad.

This all had to be done before we went to school so we had to get up very early in order to get it all done before the bus arrived to pick us up for school.

I told mom about my visionary dream in the morning and how very real it was. She was just as astonished as I was and couldn't imagine grandpa walking that route in the dark with a lantern at night and "why," because it was so unusual and not like grandpa at all.

About that same time. Grandma appeared at the door crying uncontrollably and said that grandpa was dead. She said that grandpa hadn't come in for breakfast, as he normally did after he had done a portion of the chores, so she went to see why he was gone so long. When she opened the door she found him laying on the floor and he was dead, apparently a stroke as he was having high blood pressure problems.

Then, of course, mom and I really knew what this unusual dream was all about. It just seemed to make sense. We felt that God evidently was warning us ahead of time as it really was devastating for all of us. We all have dreams, but we don't think much about them. However, some dreams are so different and so real, it's like your living them. When you wake up you just know that it has to mean something special. This dream was like that.

It was very difficult for me to get used to him not being there. He used to take me to Sunday School in his Model-T car and he let me sit in his lap and steer the car. What an experience for a girl my age. Sunday School was held at different homes each Sunday as everyone in the neighborhood took turns. After Sunday School was over, coffee was served with cake or cookies. What a great time to look forward to for the kids and parents too. That way we all got to see our neighbors at least once a week.

I can still see grandpa with white buttermilk on his dark mustache. It makes me laugh when I think about it. He was quite a grandpa!

As we get a little older we begin to realize how important our grandparents really are and have been in our growing up years. Sometimes, when we get into trouble, it was our grandparents that we felt we could cling to for a refuge, especially when we got spanked.

Those years all farmers churned their own butter and was it ever delicious. Not like today when you go to the store and get a pound of butter that has been homogenized, pasturized, diluted and colored and whatever else they do to it. But, I guess, it's supposed to be better for us.

We had a machine called a separator that we turned by hand that separated the cream from the milk. Then, when you wanted butter, you hand-turned a barrel type wood churn until you had real butter and the buttermilk that grandpa liked so well. No wonder he liked it as it was so fresh and undiluted.

In later years after I was married, I remember my husband's mother making lots of butter and selling it. They owned a "dairy farm" and sold milk products commercially. Her pounds of butter looked like small one-pound footballs and she decorated the tops with pressed designs. Even today my daughter remarks about the butter footballs and the good times she had on weekends that we spent on the dairy farm.

Grandfather, Andrew Troppi
The first of the family's
immigrants to arrive from the country of "Finland."
(1899-1900)

Chapter 5

Angel In Emergency Situation

There were, of course, many other jobs on the farm that had to be done every day and all through the year, especially during the summer growing season, like planting and harvesting cucumbers, green beans, garden produce, etc. We had a lot more time now that school was out, but there was also a lot more things that had to be done. My brother and I did everything that we could to help mom and dad. They were very good to us, and when we were through for the day, dad would take us swimming to a lake near us by the name of Healy Lake. He would take us on his "Doodle Bug", as it was called. That was really a climax for the day, and were we ever happy! The lake was about three miles away. The "Doodle Bug" was a great ride for kids. Dad had built it from an old car of some kind. No tops or sides, more like a flatbed with an engine and four wheels. Dad was very creative and had a real imagination. He had his own blacksmith shop, a separate building on the farm. When he needed a new part for his machinery, like a gear, for instance, he went into his blacksmith shop, fired up the furnace and made the part that he needed. I can still see that red hot fire where he heated and tempered his steel to make the parts.

Today, he probably would have all kinds of patents, because he even built what they call a "snowmobile" now. He often went to town on his snowmobile, which was about three miles away, especially when the roads were impassable due to the heavy snowfall, and we had a lot of it at times. We have some pictures that show us standing on top of the high banks along the side of the road. It shows us looking down at an old Model-T on the road that looked more like a midget than a car. Now, those are high banks. Talk about "global warming." I guess we had it then already, only I think it was more like "global cooling" instead.

Anyway, during those years, when things were so hard and difficult, and dad was still recuperating from his accident, and mom was so very, very ill with asthma, that God stepped in to ease our problems and their suffering. He knew, of course, what we were going through as young children with the cares and burdens that we had each day. I knew at an early age that God really loved us. But, in my mind, I questioned, "why are things so hard?"

It's hard for an eight year old to comprehend or understand why mom and dad were both so sick.

I remember how afraid I was that mom was going to die, especially when she was just gasping for air. At that time, so many years ago, there were very few medications that helped relieve asthma. I can still remember the incense odor that permeated the whole house when an incense candle was lit. It helped relieve the asthma for a few hours. The doctor had also given her adrenaline shots and showed her how to administer her own injections if she could not breathe without them.

This one particular evening, mom was sitting in front of the oven and having a terrible time breathing. She felt that the warm air from the heated oven helped her to breathe.

During this time, while I was sitting on the edge of my bed praying and sobbing to God that my mother would not die, God stepped in to ease a child's fear! That is when an angel like a clear white image appeared at the end of my bed. The angel said, "Don't worry, your mother is going to be okay." Then, she disappeared. Even though I had prayed so hard, I had no idea how God would respond or that he would send an angel! I was stunned, but really happy and relieved that mom was going to live! Can you imagine the shock and the exhilaration at that moment!

Mother had talked to me about God and heaven, and at one time even said, "When I do go to heaven, I 'm going to ask God why I had to suffer so much and for so long. I prayed, believed, and didn't get better for a long time". Knowing mom, I'm sure she did ask God about the suffering when she entered heaven, or at least intended to. However, it may not have been that important once she saw God!

The doctors had said that the main reason for the asthma was dust of any kind. Especially, grains and hay, which were the mainstay of farming. However, she always did what she could. The asthma had caused emphysema and other health problems. But, as the years went by, she did improve, was healed, and lived to be 76 years old.

We are all, the whole family, very thankful to God for intervening and helping all of us when we really needed Him the most!

Chapter 6

Farm "House Fire"

After a few years, when I was about 12, and mom and dad were somewhat better health-wise, this series of events took place. At this particular time of the day, they were both in the back 40 acres (of the 120 acres) working and were able to see what was going on. Thank God for that!

Mother had a friend over making donuts and I was helping her. She made them by mother's recipe for home-made donuts and were they ever delicious.

We had a huge old style iron cooking stove. The kind with a large "water boiler" section on the right side of the stove so you always had a large amount of hot water. Mom's friend, Irene, evidently had the stove over-heated and it set the chimney on fire. By the time we were aware of it, the embers had set the roof on fire in three different locations. It was a large two story house with a porch landing on the first floor and a ladder extending to the roof from that area. There was no electricity at that time to the outlying farms, as no electric poles or lines had been constructed as yet, so all the water had to be pumped by hand. A hard muscle building task, especially for children as young as we were, pumping all the water required for the cows and horses was quite a task as well.

Therefore, as you can visualize, Irene and I were faced with a huge challenge trying to save the house from being burned down. Irene pumped the water into large buckets and handed them to me. I had to put towels into the buckets in order to be able to douse each fire section simultaneously in order to control each area from spreading. I was running up and down from the ground to the roof top hauling those heavy buckets of water as fast as I could in order to try to control the flames.

Later on, after I had time to realize what was and had been happening, I couldn't even remember all the climbing up and down because of the trauma involved.

During this time, mom and dad had seen the flames and were heading home as fast as they could with the team of horses. By the time that they got to the house, the fires were pretty much under control outside, but they wondered what was going on inside the house. They immediately headed for the second floor to see if fires had started to burn upstairs. The fire had burned holes through the roof in three places, but hadn't spread significantly, so they were able to contain the fires and keep them from spreading any further.

What an experience this was for all of us. All I could think of afterwards was, "thank God for helping and giving us the wisdom of using wet soaked towels," as we would never have been able to get it under control otherwise. There just would not have been enough water, and we could not have been able to pump and carry it fast enough with the fire burning in three different areas.

Mom and dad were elated and thankful for what we had done. I still thank God in my heart today for saving our home! What a disaster that would have been had it burned to the ground with everything in it that they had been able to accumulate during those "Depression Years."

A traumatic experience like that burns a memory into your brain that never leaves!

There again, I know that God was in control. Maybe even with his angels, as I could have very easily slipped and fallen, especially as the water had made the shingles and everything around us so wet and slippery.

Chapter 7

Service in World War II

I was attending Michigan State University when "Pearl Harbor" was hit by the Japanese. I don't know how my parents could afford it, but as I wanted to go so bad, they found a way to help me. However, by the next term I had to leave, as I didn't have any money for books, and I just couldn't ask my parents for any more. At that time, and that age, I really felt that my life's dreams were over as I wanted to go to college so bad. It wasn't like today where there are so many ways to get help. I was working in a private home for my room and board, otherwise I wouldn't have been able to even start attending college. They gave me a little spending money weekly, but it wasn't in time to purchase books for that term.

Harvey and I were going together at the time. He was working in Battle Creek, which was about 100 miles away, and he agreed to pick me up. My father and brother were also working in Battle Creek at the time, so that is where I went too. I started to work at the Kellogg Foundation and really liked it. Harvey worked at the Eaton Manufacturing Company. We both had good interesting jobs. But, as the war was on, Harvey got drafted and had to leave. He was sent to Lawton, Oklahoma's Military Base. Since we had planned on getting married before too long, it seemed like a good time so that I could follow him wherever he went and see the country at the same time. That is what we did. We had a military wedding and it was very nice. Of course, mom and dad could not be there, neither could Harvey's parents, as it was so far away and inconvenient for them.

I met a girl on the train on the way down to Oklahoma. She also lived in Battle Creek. We seemed to have a lot in common, and got to know each other pretty well. She was going there, as her husband had also been deployed to the Lawton Army Base. That made it really nice, and they stood up for us when we got married. It was a pretty big wedding as all the servicemen that Harvey had gotten to know attended, as well as other people we had gotten acquainted with, and people from the restaurant where I was working.

Betty and I roomed together and it worked out quite well. My job was in a large restaurant with white tablecloths, so you know that it was a unique place. I really liked it and made good tips. That, of course, helped out a lot as the military wages at that time were not very much.

After about six months at that base, Harvey called and said that he could not come in anymore, as they were being shipped out. He didn't know, of course, where he was going, as no one is allowed to tell them. I really felt abandoned at the time because I didn't know where he was going or if he would be sent overseas. Here I was in basically a strange state all by myself.

After about two weeks, he called me and said that he was at a camp in Mississippi. Then, he added, "don't come here as there is absolutely no place to stay. The camp holds about 120,000 soldiers, and they all have relatives or visitors at certain times. Therefore, there are no hotels, motels, or any rooms available anywhere."

As I mentioned, I felt so abandoned being left alone in a strange state that I didn't pay too much attention to what he was saying, and felt sure that I could find some place to stay. So, I took a bus to Mississippi. Well, I guess that was a mistake! When I arrived, late in the evening, I tagged a cab and got in. He asked me, "Where do you want to go?" I said, "To a hotel." I can still remember how emphatically he said, "Lady, there ain't no hotels, motels, or any place that has any rooms." Of course, I could hardly believe my ears and said, "There has to be something. I just got here from Oklahoma and have to have a room." He didn't know what to say and pondered for awhile and said, "I'll call my aunt and see if she can do anything." Well, I ended up staying in her living room for about two weeks until I was able to locate a room some place else. So it did work out after all.

In the meantime, I looked for a job. At that time, the wages were unbelievably low, like 25 cents an hour in the factories. I don't know about other places, probably about the same.

One day I got a cab for some reason, and the cab driver started asking me questions. During the conversation, I told him I was looking for a job, and that I had just recently arrived in town as my husband was in the service at that camp. "Oh," he said, they are looking for cab drivers and can't find any, as all the men are in the service." Well, that was good news in a way, as I really needed a job. They hired me on the spot, and I was driving my own cab after two days of training. I thought to myself, 'whew, what have I done?' But, in a way, I felt I was doing my part for the war effort too, and that part made me feel good!

Boy, was I scared! My first trip was to get someone from the train depot and then just come back to the cab station. The train depot seemed so desolate and it was hard to find a location where someone would be waiting for a cab. I can still remember how hard it was for me to keep my foot on the gas peddle as it was shaking so hard. What an experience that first trip was! I was only twenty years old at the time.

But, after a few weeks, I even told my husband that I really liked the job, and I did get good tips. It wasn't like working for 25 cents an hour.

He was quite furious at first when I told him what I was doing. However, he cooled down before too long, and even enjoyed riding with me when he was on leave or could get off to spend some time in town.

It was the Yellow Cab Company. They had two twelve hour shifts. The girls drove during the day and the men drove at night, seven days a week, 6 a.m. to 6 p.m.

It was really different driving a cab at that time as there were no cell phones, not even any phone booths. They had erected telephone set-ups attached to telephone poles in various places in town. We had to stop at these poles and call in to check if we had a pick-up to bring back to the station or somewhere else on our way back. That was our only way of communication to find out what we had to do next. Sounds like ancient history, doesn't it? But, that was only in the 1940's, really not that long ago!

The wars lasted from 1942 to 1945.

At that time, a lot of things had to be purchased with coupons. You only received a certain amount. You soon learned what food to buy and how much gas you were able to get. You didn't have gas for pleasure trips, etc., as you do today, and they only gave you the necessary amount of gas coupons for your situation, and we all just had to watch it!

However, one day I did end up in a court situation, which was a mind-boggling experience for someone that had grown up so sheltered and protected from the world's conditions and lavish exuberance of those decades. My intellect was awakened in a hurry and I felt a lot more grown up after my court experience.

What happened was, the lady I picked up had a baby with her, and a big brown bag full of empty bottles. During the trip she was holding the baby in her arms while sitting in the back seat. All of a sudden, she let the baby fall on the floor and made no gestures or effort to pick her up. I stopped the cab and put the baby back into her arms, and then proceeded traveling towards our destination. When we got downtown, she wanted to stop at the bank. However, there were no parking spots available, so I had to double park while she went in. She went into the bank, took the baby with her, and said that she would be right back. However, she was gone a very long time, and I didn't know what to do. I couldn't leave the cab while I was double parked. At that very moment a gentlemen got in and asked to go to a different location. I told him I couldn't leave until the lady that went into the bank returned, and that she had been gone a very long time. He agreed to go into the bank and see if there was a lady there that had a baby with her. He came back shortly and said there was no lady in the bank that had a baby with her. So I continued taking him to his destination and then returned to the cab station. When I got back, I told them exactly what had transpired. They already knew quite a bit about it, as the police had picked her up for some reason and were at the station.

Before long, I had a summons to appear in court to explain the whole situation as to what had transpired that day. I later learned that she was a captain's wife, and that there was an injunction and court hearing scheduled concerning her capability of being a fit mother, and that there was a possibility they would take the baby away from her.

I never found out how the court hearing turned out, but it certainly was an awakening and educational experience for a 20 year old.

After Harvey had been in Mississippi for about a year, he was having trouble with asthma, especially when he had to go on those twenty-five mile hikes. He would end up with an asthma attack and just couldn't make it. He was sent to the hospital several times. Consequently, after a period of time, he received an honorable discharge.

He then went back to his previous job in Battle Creek at the Eaton Manufacturing Company, and I went back to work at Kellogg's. However, being that it was during the war and help was hard to get, his parents wanted him to work on their dairy farm for awhile. We spent about a year there helping them out. Then we moved to Muskegon, about 100 miles away, and both worked at the Norge Division. They had taken on the responsibility of making airplane wings and related equipment for the Air Force. They too had a hard time getting enough help. That is why we went there because we heard they needed help so desperately. At one time while working there, I was a riveter on one side of the airplane wing, and another person was on the other side. It was what you would call a "shaking and jarring" experience. They called us girls "Rosie, the Riveters." I worked there for about 5 years and then went back to college. The war, of course, was over by that time. Harvey stayed there for about 17 years as a shift supervisor.

Harvey felt that he did all he could for the war effort and for as long as he could. I was not, of course, in the service, but I too felt that I did what I could... driving a cab and working on airplane wings. There just were not enough men around to do these jobs, as so many had to be in the service. After all, we were fighting two wars at one time. Everyone had to dig in and do what they could! Many of our friends and schoolmates died fighting for our country. They paid the ultimate sacrifice! We still miss them, especially when we go to our Class Reunions and "they are remembered." Even though it was so long ago, it still hurts.

This is briefly our story during a time that our country was in two wars at one time. Probably the only time in history that it seemed like we were fighting the whole world in order to keep our freedom! But, we are still "FREE!"

There were thousands and thousands of other couples that were in similar situations, as well as many of our family members. But, our greatest thanks goes to the servicemen and women that gave their ultimate sacrifice for our freedom! How can we be grateful enough!

Chapter 8

God's Healings

We know that God can heal and does heal because of his Word and two separate instances in our own family, but both were after many, many years of suffering. Many things are so hard to understand. We know our faith is weak, but everything is done at God's timing, not ours, and he has his reasons. Like the Bible tells us in Matthew 17 that if we had the faith of a mustard seed {the smallest of all seeds}, we could move mountains. "By God's power, of course." It means there is no limit to what He can do or accomplish in our lives.

I covered most of mom's problems, allergies, etc. in another chapter. Farming, of course, was not conducive to her health and lifestyle. But, how would a person know ahead of time that she would have those kinds of problems. After all, her parents had no other options, but farming, when they started their new lifestyle in this new country, at least to begin with.

My mother was healed after many years of severe asthma and related problems. I know from what she said about God and healing, and studying his word, that she was healed. She lived for many healthy years after that. She believed and received.

In our own immediate family, our son had very severe asthma from a baby on until he was 14 years old. He was very small and thin for a 14 year old. I remember when I took him into Emergency at the hospital when he was less than a year old. He was very white and ill when I got there. They made me wait in line, even though he was so ill. Then he passed out in my arms. Just at that very moment our family doctor's nurse walked by and saw what was happening. She had the doctor there in seconds. He grabbed him and said,"he will be okay," trying to assure me, I'm sure. Besides that, it was our own family doctor that knew all about him and his condition, not some other doctor at the hospital that would not have known anything about him and his problems.

It turned out that he was allergic to the medicine they had given him for the asthma. If it had been another doctor, the circumstances could have been much different. I knew right then that God intervened and sent our doctor's nurse there just at the right moment. What a God we have! What a blessing that was! God knows our every move long before we do.

Allergies are usually the cause of asthma and our son was no exception. We had problems with his formula right from the beginning. We found out as time went on that he had many allergies. We even tried the allergy shots that were specifically formulated for him, but they didn't work and actually made him worse.

To make a long story short, he had a lot of problems with food and medicines. He had pneumonia a couple of times, which wasn't unusual with all of his problems.

One day, when he was fourteen, he had an awful attack of asthma. We took him to the doctor's office immediately. He treated him for four hours between patients and even administered adrenaline and watched him closely until he improved. This was a very traumatic day.

The doctor then pulled us aside and talked to us about his condition. What he told us was astonishing. He said that he already had a touch of emphysema in his lungs even though he was only fourteen. Then he added, " if he continues this way, he would be in a wheelchair by the time he is twenty-five years old." This about blew us away!

My daughter told me just last year that she remembers, when we came home from the doctor, that I was pounding my head against the wall. I remember that too because I was so traumatized over what the doctor told us. He also said that he didn't know of anything else that could be done for him other than what he had already done.

My husband and I had been praying for him right along but nothing had changed. Why, we wondered? That night when I went to bed I "really" prayed. I had not prayed so hard in all my life. I still wonder sometimes what I said to God and what promises I must have made. But, this I know, I've tried to be a good Christian. I know that my husband prayed fervently as well!

The asthma attack he had that day is the last attack he has ever had. God really answered our prayers! He is fifty-four years old now, so we know God can heal and does heal. I thank him all the time for His goodness, grace, and mercy, and for loving us all so much more than we can ever realize, and certainly don't deserve. What a "Blessing" he gave our son, and all of us too!

After that he started feeling much better in every way. He did better in school and began to enjoy life! He started growing as well. Then we wondered when he was going to stop growing, and if he was going to be the world's tallest man! Well, he didn't stop growing until he was almost 6'7" tall. The doctor told us that it was probably because of all the steroids that he had to have to control his asthma that no doubt contributed to his height, as there was no one in our family line that was over 6' tall.

Angels are in our thought life as well. They do not have to appear and talk to us to be effective in our lives. God sends them at will to do what he wants done.

Even in this instance in the Emergency Room at the hospital, I saw no visible angel or angels, but the situation certainly had to be guided by God, as the nurse and doctor were there at those very specific "seconds" when they were so desperately needed. The timing definitely saved our son's life!

Of course, coincidental situations do occur, but I am convinced this was God's intervention directly by him or through his angels when seconds counted! The Bible does say in Psalms 91 that God shall give his angels "charge" over us and keep us in all our ways.

I do admonish that God's angels are here on earth for our benefit doing whatever the Lord wants done in our personal and spiritual lives. Many situations that have occurred in the world over past centuries verify they exist and perform his will!

Chapter 9

The Holy Spirit in our Lives

It was in the late 1970's that the church that our daughter and her husband attended had what was called a Lay Witness Mission. Many people from various denominations came to their church and gave account of what had happened in their lives by what would have to be described as a supernatural event. They told of many spontaneous healings and interventions that do not normally occur. They had experienced the same type of events that the bible talks about, but these things were happening to them now. There was a refreshing taking place in the church and even though we had always gone to church, we didn't know that kind of thing could or would happen in our lives when we needed help. To these people, it didn't seem to matter which church you belonged to or exactly how you practiced your faith, just that God was as real today as he was in bible times.

After our daughter did some research on the acts of the Holy Spirit, she too came to believe that God works and moves the same today and will help us when we go to him believing he is there for us personally.

She shared this Spirit-led way of life with her brother first and he also experienced some direct interventions of help for some problems that he had no control over, which began to change his life for the better and make God real to him.

My husband and I were watching our children change and seeing the reality of God in our daily lives. The presence of the Holy Spirit was becoming more real as each day went by. It was the beginning of a completely new way of living.

We began to study more and to pray more together as a family. It really made a big difference. We just felt so much closer to God, especially during our prayer sessions. We began to understand much more clearly how the Holy Spirit works and functions in our daily lives.

We began to realize that when we reach out to God, He reaches out to us even more. It is like an awakening of the Holy Spirit working and dwelling in our lives, making changes in our mind and in our heart, just becoming more alive.

God has given each one of us certain "Gifts of the Spirit," and talents. As Christians, He expects us to use these gifts and talents to the best of our ability.

He gave us our first breath and He will give us our last breath. In the interim period of our lives, He wants us to do "His Will" to the best of our capability here on earth.

Chapter 10

Armored Angels
Best Christian Friend

This was a revelation from God I will never forget!

Kathy was the best friend that I ever had. We loved talking about God and what being Spirit-filled meant. We would both be so joyful and happy that we were able to share God's love and scripture together. We just seemed to understand how each other felt.

We were both in a "helping others" business environment that just made you feel good. She had some health problems and was searching about a "spirit-filled" relationship with God.

One day my friend Judy said, "How about coming to our Sunday evening service tonight?" It was a very different type of church service than I had ever been to before, but, I said, "I'll be there." I called Kathy to see if she would like to go and she said, "I'll drive, I'll pick you up at six." I said,"great." I went into the back bedroom to get ready and the almost unbelievable happened. I was in a hurry as it wouldn't be long before she would be there. She only lived about a mile away. As I was rushing back and forth through the house, I looked out the front door to see if she was already in the driveway. She wasn't.

However, just as clearly as could be, I saw two men dressed in full body armor, complete with head helmets, breast plates, and body armor coming up the steps to the front door. But, when they got to the top of the steps, they just vanished, they were gone! It was so astounding, I could hardly believe my eyes, but it was real! It was like I was looking at them in front of my eyes. I knew they had to be angels sent by God for some reason. Why else would they have been there just at that moment. I questioned in my mind, "how come, and why right now when I was in such a hurry getting ready? And why the armor? And why did they just disappear when they got to the top of the steps?

I shared this with Kathy on the way to the church service. She could hardly believe what she was hearing and asked me to go over it all again so she could grasp it all. She was just flabbergasted and wondered, as I did, "how come and what did it mean!"

Well, we soon got our answers. We met Judy and her family when we got to the church and we all went in together. We were glad as we had never been there before. What a great greeting we had. They were all so glad to see us. It was a nice church and everyone was so friendly and hospitable. We met the pastor and his wife and thought they were great people.

To our astonishment, the whole service was, "Put on the whole armor of God that you may be able to stand against the wiles of the devil." (Ephesians 6-11). We were both in awe knowing that God was at work, somehow teaching us something, but what? We both had a lot to think and pray about. I certainly learned a lot and was so glad that Kathy was there as she had met with me many times questioning and asking about the Holy Spirit and the spirit-filled life.

I was in my 60's and Kathy was about ten years younger at the time. It wasn't very long after this event that our home sold. We moved North about 100 miles away. I knew that I would really miss her as she was my best friend, but it wasn't so far that I wouldn't see her once in awhile.

We had purchased this old lakefront lodge a few years earlier in anticipation of remodeling it for our retirement home. We both enjoyed rebuilding and remodeling homes. It was a large seven bedroom former Bed and Breakfast Lodge and needed a lot of work. We remodeled the whole building, ending up with a four bedroom, three bath home, with the front area housing a store. We really enjoyed it and got our exercise as well. Many couples that were in our pinochle club visited us frequently. That is, just about every weekend. Being on the lake was an asset in many ways and enjoyable for all of us.

I didn't see Kathy as much as I would have liked to, but she was busy with her business and we, of course, were busy remodeling.

I knew that she was having health problems but I didn't know how serious they were. Then, one day, a friend of mine called and said that she had died. That was a terrible shock! Somehow I just knew or felt that the event revealing the armored angels and the church service was God working in his mysterious ways, as the Bible states, and he had planned it for increasing our faith. Only God knows the reasons, when, how, and where, to help strengthen our faith in Him.

I sure miss her but feel so blessed and fortunate God put her in my life for so many joyful, happy, and learning experiences! She was still so young when she passed away, but in her business and short life, she had been a blessing to so many, many people!

We had held weekly business meetings together on personal business building techniques, proven inspirational data in other various businesses, and gathered informational aspects of other successful businesses. Breakfast meetings on the weekends were especially well attended and enjoyed by all attendees. It was a lot of work but educational, rewarding, and inspirational helping others to build their businesses and future. It was a part-time business for us, as it was in addition to our full time jobs.

Chapter 11

An Angel's Appearance

Just a few years before our house sold and we moved North, this event took place. When I was in the bedroom making my bed, an angelic being walked/flowed through my room. She wasn't doing anything, or looking anywhere, just going straight ahead. She came in one side and went out the other side of the room. This seemed so strange. I felt sort of stunned and over-whelmed. What was the purpose? There had to be a reason that God sent an angel right then, but what and why? I wondered and pondered for about a week and nothing seemed to make any sense.

That coming weekend we went up North, about 100 miles away, where both of us were brought up and where both of our parents and families still resided. Some of our siblings had moved away but our parents still lived there. My husband's parents lived in a small town by the name of Onekama, and my parents lived about ten miles further north in a small town by the name of Kaleva, so it was nice and convenient to see all of the relatives at the same time so we didn't have to make two trips to see all of them.

After arriving there we found out that one of his brothers was very ill and in the hospital. He wasn't expected to live very long. This was a shock as we didn't know anything about it. I guess it came on suddenly and they had not had a chance to call us to let us know. We went to the hospital immediately to see him and, of course, the whole family was there at his bedside. At that time we both felt like there was a heavy load on us for some reason. We discussed it and even though as a child his brother had been baptized and went to Sunday School every Sunday, we wondered if he had been saved. At that very moment we both felt that this must be the reason God had sent an angel to warn us or administer to us and to tell us that we had a job to do, after all this was his brother, and if there was anything we could do, we better do it. Of course, the only thing we really could do was to pray.

When we saw the family, we expressed our concern over his condition and sympathy that he was so ill. After awhile we left and told them that we would be back in a little while to see how he was.

After leaving and we were about a mile down the road, I told my husband, "We have to go back. I don't know why, but we have to go back now." So we turned around and went back to the hospital. He was in a coma by that time, and we told the family that we came back because we felt that we had to pray with him. However, since he was in a coma we didn't know for sure what to do as he couldn't hear us or respond. Now, we know, that someone in that condition probably can hear. We were not sure what to do so we talked to his wife saying, "For some reason after leaving we felt that we had to come back and pray for him." She said, "Fine, but don't say anything that would hurt him." "Of course, we won't," we said, but for some reason it just didn't seem to fit in with him in a coma and with the whole family there, so we decided to talk to her again. We explained the situation to her and told her that since he was not responsive at that time, we would not pray for him at the hospital. However, we would leave and go into intercessory prayer for him. She said, "that would be fine." We could see that she was more at ease and we all felt better. We knew that was God leading us to do the right thing at the right time. We did pray for him, especially for his salvation and forgiveness of sins. We thanked God for his intervention and guiding us to do what we felt he wanted us to do. It wasn't long and he went home to be with the Lord. The Bible tells us that God works in mysterious ways. We wanted to be obedient and do what we felt God was leading us to do, and that must have been the reason why the angel had appeared. My husband felt much better afterwards. After all, this was one of his brothers. He wanted to be obedient and considerate to his brother's family at the same time.

Illustration by
Great Grand-daughter Emma Thompson

Chapter 12

What Do Angels Look Like?

I can understand that people that have not seen angels are curious as to what they really look like. It's quite difficult to explain as their appearance is so instantaneous. Especially the first time, I was so stunned and overwhelmed at that instant that I was not making any visual characterization of what was really happening.

I can only say that at the first two instances they appeared to be female. I saw them only from a frontal view. They were like white translucent angels, not brilliant, pretty much as normally characterized in pictures, which are probably portrayed from other appearances. I did not see wings, as often portrayed, but they would have been on the back anyway. I don't believe they need wings as they can probably move thousands of miles in seconds.

In the third appearance, there were two of them, and they were in full metal armor. My impression is that they looked male in appearance. However, the spirit realm is different. Angels have their assignments by God. Is gender relevant?

Chapter 13

PRAYER
How Do You Pray?

One of our neighbors was having a lot of trouble health-wise. She had always been very faithful attending her church all of her life. One day she asked my son to pray for her husband as he was very ill. She said, "I don't know how to pray." Our son was dumb-founded and said, "What do you mean, you don't know how to pray? You are very faithful in going to church." "Yes, but they don't teach us or tell us how to pray. They just have a church service." He, of course, was very willing, and did pray for her husband.

Our son said, "He is your heavenly father! All you have to do is talk to him. Tell him how you feel and what you need, just like you are talking to me or anyone else. It's as simple as that! He listens, he hears, he even knows beforehand what you need and what you are going to say. Prayer is being in communion with God."

After that, she seemed to feel much better about the situation, and seemed to be more at ease. Our son went over many times after that, as it was a close neighbor, prayed and helped in any way that he could.

(Reference: Philippians Ch. 4-6-7)

Chapter 14

A Revealing God

My husband, Harvey, passed away in February, 2009, at the age of 87, after several years of varying complications, such as, arthritis, heart surgery, hip surgery, knee replacement, fistula and gall bladder surgery. He certainly had a lot of problems, and we feel this all started with a brown recluse spider bite, which many times is fatal. During the last two to three years he had intermittent heart fibrillations which gradually weakened his heart. Each time that he was in the hospital, we all tried to be there as much as we could to keep him company and pray for him.

However, this one particular time when he was very ill, we had a real different type of revelation of God's presence and power in our lives. God has given all of us spiritual gifts of some nature but it's hard to really know what they are and how to use them to best fit God's purposes, but, of course, we all do our best.

God has blessed both our daughter and our son, with a very unique spiritual gift of prayer. We have all noticed it many times, especially at very needful circumstances.

At this one particular time, Harvey was in the hospital for triple by-pass surgery. He was out of surgery but was coherent and able to talk to us. In this instance, our son said that he was going to pray for dad. He stood at the end of his bed and began to pray. It wasn't a planned prayer. It was in his own words from the heart, an ad-libbed prayer. There was no way that Harvey knew what he was going to say, and it was a pretty long prayer. All of a sudden, during the prayer, Harvey began to pray simultaneously with him saying the same exact words for quite a long time. We had never encountered anything like this and it really, you might say, stunned us all. We just looked at each other and could hardly believe what we were hearing. Saying the same words at the same time had to be the Holy Spirit speaking through Harvey as there was no way that he could have known what our son was going to say. What a great God we have! It was a real revelation for everyone in the room to realize that the very presence of the Holy Spirit was with us. Like the Bible tells us, God works in mysterious ways. What a great Christian experience this was for all of us!

Chapter 15

Transition

Most people in transition just pass away and do not noticeably experience any audible sentences or gestures. However, we have all heard of many instances that were quite to the contrary, especially with some people that have had "near-death" experiences. In my husband's case, we had some audible revelations.

In 2009 when he was in the hospital and very ill, we knew that he wasn't going to make it because of his weak heart and frequent fibrillations. This resulted in very poor circulation to both of his feet. Consequently, gangrene became evident in both feet. Surgery was not a possibility because of his weakened heart.

For the last two weeks that he was with us and in the hospital, we spent as much time with him as possible. The doctors had him on pain medication to make him as comfortable as possible. Consequently, we did not know for sure when we talked to him if he heard us or not. Normally, he was a person that talked all the time and others had a hard time getting a word in. Now, for understandable reasons, he was just the opposite and it was hard to converse with him.

The nurses spent a lot of time with him and were so pleasant and congenial. That, of course, helped us a lot and made it so much easier for all of us.

The very last evening that we were with him he did talk a little more than usual. We did not know at the time that it was his last day with us. At one point, he said, "I don't know if I'm here or if I'm there," so we felt that he must have been in transition. Evidently, that was the case, as he passed away about midnight.

The nurses were very attentive and had spent a lot of time with him. We were really glad they did because they were able to tell us exactly what had transpired during his last hours. The one nurse told us that just before he passed away, he had called out a female name, and it seemed to be with some expectancy. We mentioned several names in the family, and when the name, Lena, was mentioned, she said, "that's it." That was his mother's name. From that experience, we really felt that he must have been in the last moments of his transition and saw his mother. He had never, that I know of, even mentioned his mother's name for many, many years. She had passed away about 52 years earlier.

This, to us, is really another indication and revelation of "life after death." Two things: 'I don't know if I'm here or if I'm there, and calling out his mother's name,' at the time that he passed away.

It still amazes us how calm and peaceful he was those last two weeks of his life in accepting his on-coming fate. Of course, we were glad that he was because it made it so much easier for him and for the whole family. Thank God for his grace and peace especially at those most difficult times of our lives!

I remember when he had his triple by-pass surgery four years earlier, that the hospital pastor came in to see him just before he went into surgery. The pastor remarked, " I have never seen anyone so calm and collected just before going into heart surgery." But, that was Harvey! He had accepted God a long time ago. I believe that was his peace! What a great way to be and to live. Thank God for His Grace, Peace and Blessings!

Blessings

Chapter 16

God's Blessings

I feel blessed that God has helped me especially at times in my young life when I needed his help so desperately, as you know from reading this book. However, I never could have even imagined that he would send his messengers, his angels, to answer my prayers. But, in my young years and seemingly hopeless situations, He evidently felt it necessary.

I can only say that as far back as I can remember, as a child, I felt that I always wanted to please God in everything that I did. Maybe that was his way of saying, "I hear you! I know that you believe in me, and trust me."

We all know, as Christians, as believers, that God has a purpose or plan, or plans, for everything that he does, for every one of us.

As the bible tells us, God works in his own mysterious ways to accomplish his purposes here on earth and beyond.

We, no doubt, are very carnal/worldly in our perception of God and his Son, Jesus, who suffered with horrendous pain and affliction, that we cannot even imagine. And, He did this for you and for me. How can we even comprehend the magnitude of "God's Great Love" for mankind, even with such a sacrifice!

Now, when I look back over the years of my life, I know that he had a plan for my life, as he has for every person. I believe that writing this book was a part of his plan, mainly because I felt so intensely certain that he wanted me to write it. After all, he evidently gave me the idea in the first place. Thereby, this being just another way to spread his word around the world. Possibly even to those individuals that are skeptical of the existence of a God or Supreme Being, because they feel they have no proof of his existence. Even though there has to be a God or Supreme Being that made us and all things around us, the heavens and the earth and everything that exists!

I hope and pray that these experiences are helpful to others that may be in difficult circumstances in their lives, and may now realize that there is a God that is willing to help them and is just waiting to hear from them!

Chapter 17

The Last Century
The Next Century

I'm sure, if my parents and grandparents were here today, they would have a hard time believing the advancements and accomplishments that this country, our United States of America, has made in just one century. It's almost unbelievable. There were no cars, airplanes, T.V.'s, telephones, sky-scraper buildings, huge cities like New York, Chicago, Dallas, etc. Highways of today's enormity are just fantastic. The Internet and all that it has and does and can do is just about unbelievable. The accomplishments are just mind-boggling when you really think about it!

Things, of course, that this generation just takes for granted, as it seems to them that they have always been there. That is because that is all they have ever known, seen, or experienced! That's understandable.

This has all taken place since the early 1900's. The changes in just the last two or three decades are astonishing to all of us, especially what the Internet has accomplished and is accomplishing on a daily basis! How many and what new discoveries and innovations will be instituted into our society in the next few decades? Wouldn't it be interesting to know ahead of time!

The Lord willing, civilization and the world still exists for many more decades. I hope and pray that the spiritual events categorized in the bible, especially in the book of "Revelations," will help to maximize the morality and minimize the immorality that exists so prevalently in our society today... before Jesus returns!

Chapter 18

Believers And Non-Believers

For those of you who, in your mind, question the existence of a God or Supreme Being, I hope that by reading this book, and the "revelations" revealed in this book, will help and guide you in your controversial search for spiritual wisdom, and for answers relative to your life.

As mentioned in a previous chapter, there are believers and non-believers in the "enormity of a higher power." Someone or something had to have created everything that exists. How did it happen?

To begin with, the billions or trillions of space or spaciousness, as we call it, exists without a doubt. The planets in the total universe, how many are there? Or, how many could there be? Civilization has no clue as to what all really and truly exists in that spaciousness.

We know of some, the sun and the moon that give us light. If they didn't exist, there wouldn't be anything but darkness. That would be something, wouldn't it? Then, for sure, there would be no life, as life wouldn't or couldn't exist in complete darkness all the time. Where did they come from?

Then, there are planets, like the Earth, Mars, Jupiter, Stars, etc., as we call them. How did they form? Something had to form them or they wouldn't exist and be a reality. But, we know they exist!

Then, how about us human beings? Some "Magnificent Entity," with a mind-boggling brain and ability had to exist that could create the first human being. A person with eyes that can see, ears that can hear, heart that pumps blood, veins, arteries, nerves, cells, etc. All in the right order and in the right place. Legs so it can walk, arms so it can do things...a "human being."

That "Magnificent Spiritual Entity" that created all of this is what we call "God!" Our Heavenly Father!

"Angelic Visits Today"

written by

Helmi L. Schimke

Compiled by
Sally Koon
Jackpine Business Centers
Manistee, Michigan
July, 2011

Cover Color and Title by
Helmi Schimke